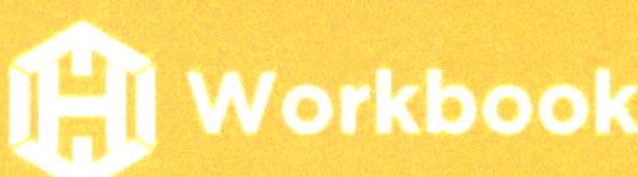

2024

THE MODEL HANDBOOK

Your Essential Guide to Breaking into the Industry

Author By
Sara Vargas

Table of
CONTENTS

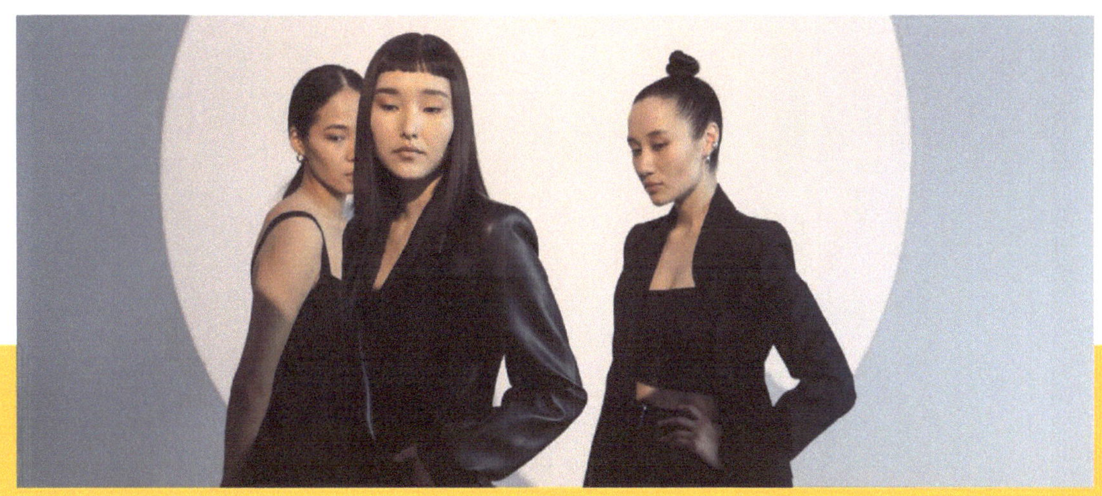

Introduction

Welcome to the Glamorous World of Modeling

Whether you're dreaming of strutting down runways, gracing magazine covers, or even becoming the next meme sensation, the modeling world is your oyster. So, buckle up, buttercup, because we're about to take a wild ride through the wild and wacky world of commercial, fashion and fierce poses!

Now, let me paint you a picture: the flash of cameras, the sound of heels clacking, the smell of hairspray and dreams—okay, maybe not the last one, but you get the idea. It's a world where every step is a strut, every pose is a statement, and every outfit is a masterpiece. But beware, my friend, for amidst the glitter and glamour lies a land of trials, tribulations, and occasional wardrobe malfunctions. Yes, even supermodels have their moments of "oops, did I just trip over my own feet?" But fear not, for with a sprinkle of confidence and a dash of sass, you'll conquer the modeling world like a boss.

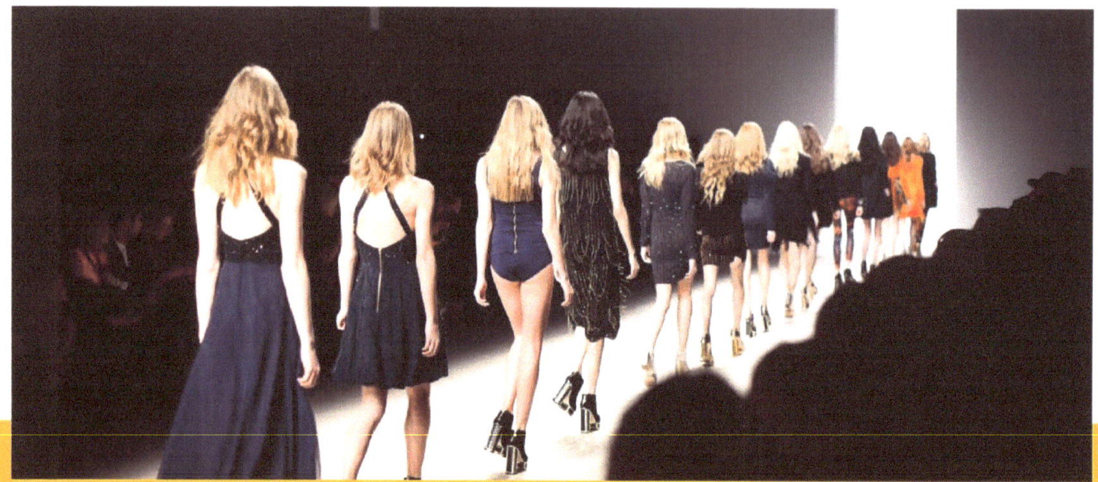

But before we dive headfirst into the chaos and couture, let's take a moment to map out our path to world domination—err, I mean, modeling success. In the chapters to come, we'll uncover the mysteries of modeling genres, decode the secrets of stunning portfolios, and navigate the treacherous waters of auditions with all the grace and elegance of a swan on a Segway.

So, grab your heels, strike a pose, and get ready to unleash your inner diva, because honey, this is going to be one heck of a ride!

To-Do List:
- Dive into research on at least three different modeling genres, and remember, it's okay to have more than one favorite—variety is the spice of life!
- Reflect on your strengths and passions to determine which modeling path suits you best. And hey, if you're still figuring it out, that's okay too—life's a catwalk, not a sprint!
- Create a vision board or journal to capture your wildest dreams and aspirations. Who knows, maybe one day you'll look back and laugh at how far you've come—from dreamer to runway ruler!

Chapter 1

Unveiling the Diverse World of Modeling

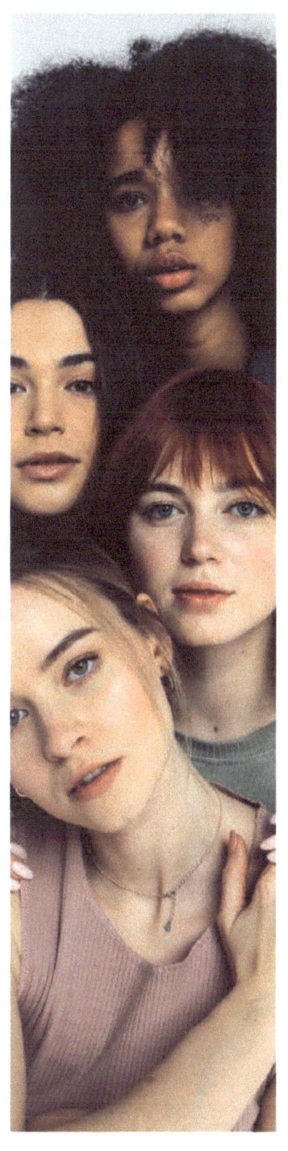

Exploring Modeling Genres

Okay, let's talk about modeling genres. Picture this: it's like a buffet of fabulousness, with something for everyone! Whether you're into high fashion, commercial gigs, or fitness modeling, there's a place for you in this crazy world of modeling. Let's break it down:

- **Fashion Modeling:** Ah, the cream of the crop! Fashion modeling is all about strutting your stuff on the catwalk and gracing the glossy pages of top magazines.

- **Commercial Modeling:** Now, this is where the real people shine! Commercial modeling is all about representing everyday folks and showing off products in ads and commercials. It's relatable, it's accessible, and it's oh-so-much fun!

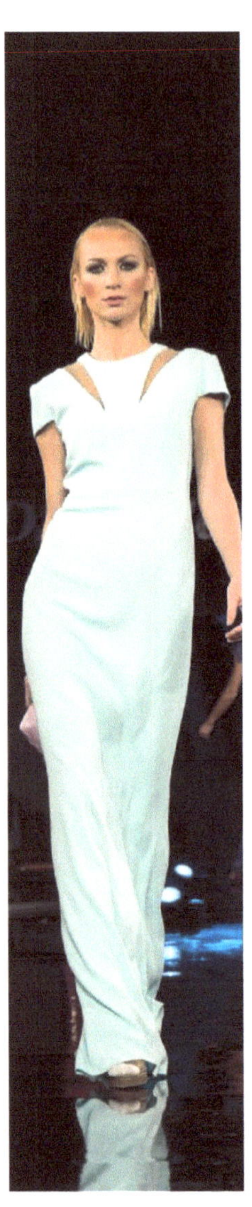

- **Fitness Modeling:** Get ready to break a sweat! Fitness modeling is all about promoting health and wellness and inspiring others to get moving. Whether you're a yoga guru or a CrossFit fanatic, there's a place for you in the world of fitness modeling.

- **Glamour Modeling:** Ooh la la! Glamour modeling is all about embracing your inner bombshell and celebrating the beauty of the human form. From lingerie shoots to nude portraits, it's all about confidence, sass, and plenty of attitude.

- **Social Media Modeling:** Social media models are very popular in this day an age, these model use social media as a tool to showcase user generated content for brands that have an online presence.

- **Editorial Modeling:** Last but not least, we have editorial modeling. This is where the magic happens, folks! Editorial models bring stories to life in the pages of magazines, embodying characters and emotions with every pose.

Personalized Questions:

Now, let's get personal! Here are some questions to help you navigate your modeling journey:

- Which modeling niches are you most interested in exploring? (Fashion, commercial, fitness, glamour, editorial, Instagram, etc.)

- Have you researched local modeling agencies in your area? List them here.

- What are your strengths as a model? (e.g., confidence, versatility, photogenic, etc.) List them below.

- What areas do you feel you need to improve upon? (e.g., runway skills, posing techniques, networking, etc.) Be honest with yourself and jot down your weaknesses.

- Do you have any specific goals or milestones you'd like to achieve in your modeling career? Write them down and let's make them happen!

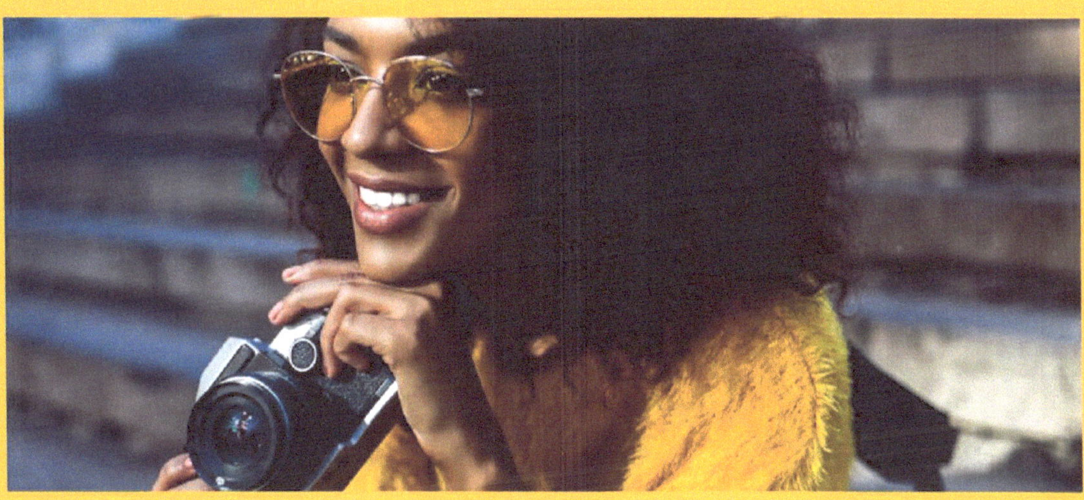

Discovering Your Modeling Niche

Now that we've covered the basics, it's time to find your niche in this crazy world of modeling. But don't worry, I've got your back! Here are a few tips to help you on your way:

- **Reflect on Your Strengths and Passions:** Think about what gets your heart racing and your creative juices flowing. Are you a fashionista at heart, or do you feel more at home in front of the camera promoting products?

- **Experiment and Explore:** Don't be afraid to try new things and step out of your comfort zone. Take on different gigs, work with different photographers, and see what feels right for you.

- **Seek Guidance and Mentorship:** We're all in this together, so don't be afraid to reach out for help and advice. Connect with experienced models and industry insiders who can share their wisdom and support you on your journey.

- **Stay True to Yourself:** Above all else, remember to stay true to who you are. Embrace your quirks, flaunt your individuality, and let your unique personality shine through in everything you do.

As we wrap up this chapter, remember that the world of modeling is a wild and wonderful place, filled with endless possibilities and opportunities. So go ahead, dream big, work hard, and get ready to make your mark on the world. Because trust me, superstar, the best is yet to come!

notes

Chapter 2

Crafting Your Visual Story
The Power of Portfolios

Unlock the Secrets to Crafting a Captivating Portfolio

Your portfolio isn't just a collection of pretty pictures—it's your calling card, your visual story, your ticket to modeling stardom! So, let's roll up our sleeves and dive into the nitty-gritty of crafting a portfolio that'll make heads turn and jaws drop.

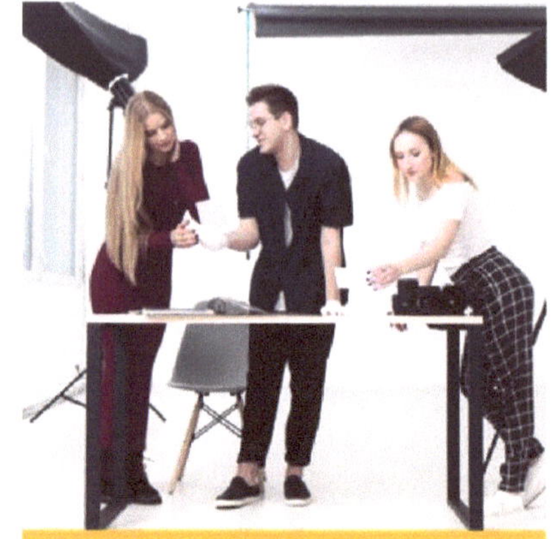

Define Your Narrative:

Before you start snapping away, take a moment to think about the story you want your portfolio to tell. Are you a chameleon, capable of morphing into any character with ease? Or maybe you're a fitness fanatic, ready to flex those muscles and show the world what you're made of. Whatever your vibe, make sure your portfolio screams "you" from every pixel.

Welcome to the second leg of our thrilling journey through the glamorous universe of modeling!

Curate with Purpose:

In a sea of selfies and snapshots, it's important to stand out from the crowd. Choose images that not only look amazing but also tell a cohesive story.

Showcase Versatility:

In the world of modeling, versatility is key. Show off your range by including a variety of shots that highlight different sides of your personality.

Quality Over Quantity:

When it comes to portfolios, it's quality, not quantity, that counts. So, instead of bombarding potential clients with a million mediocre shots, focus on a select few that really pack a punch.

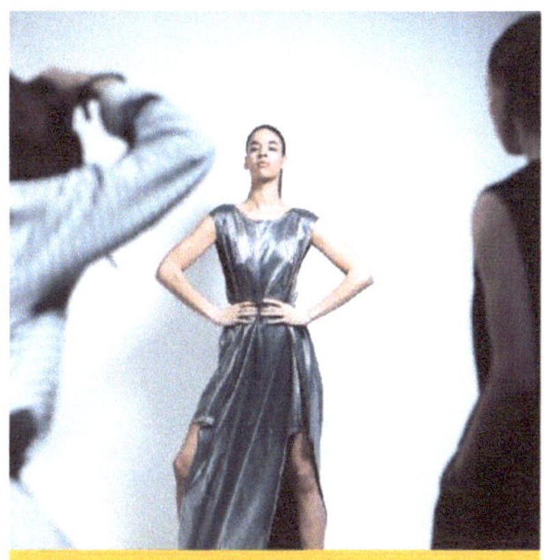

Here, amidst the swirling vortex of creativity, we're diving headfirst into the enchanting world of portfolio crafting—a realm where images become stories and dreams take flight.

Transform Your Photos into a Story That Speaks Volumes

Now that you've got your photos picked out, it's time to turn them into a narrative that'll leave people speechless. Think of your portfolio as a mini movie starring you—it should have drama, suspense, and a killer ending!

Embrace Cohesion:

A great portfolio is like a symphony—it should flow seamlessly from one image to the next. Choose photos that complement each other in terms of style, mood, and vibe, creating a visual journey that's as smooth as silk.

Sequencing Matters:

Just like a good story, your portfolio should have a beginning, a middle, and an end. Start strong, build momentum, and finish with a bang, leaving viewers wanting more.

Tell a Story:

Don't just show off your pretty face—tell a story! Whether it's the tale of your transformation from shy kid to runway superstar or the saga of your quest for world domination, let your portfolio be a window into your world.

Transform Your Photos into a Story That Speaks Volumes

Leave Them Wanting More:

End your portfolio with a showstopper that'll leave people clamoring for an encore. Choose a killer shot that encapsulates everything you're about, leaving viewers hungry for more.

As we wrap up our exploration of portfolio power, remember: your portfolio isn't just a collection of photos—it's your ticket to modeling greatness. So, take these tips, go forth, and conquer the world, one fabulous photo at a time!

To-Do List for Portfolio Perfection:

- Define the narrative or theme for your portfolio.
- Select a diverse range of high-quality images that showcase your versatility.
- Ensure cohesion and flow throughout your portfolio.
- Start and end strong, leaving a lasting impression.
- Invest in top-notch photography and styling for professional results.

notes

notes

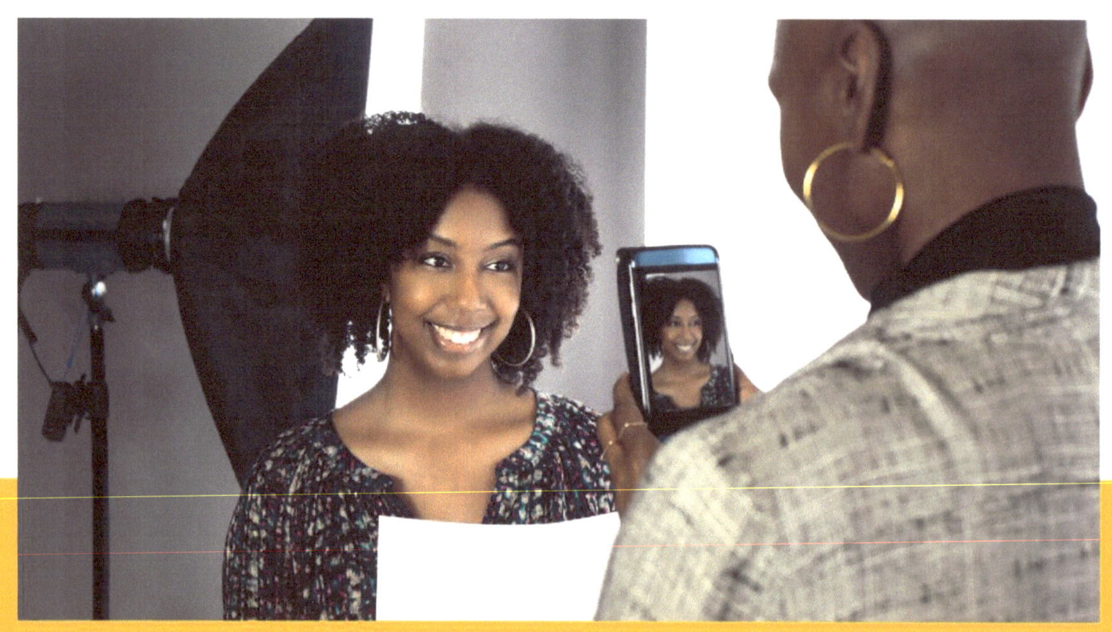

Chapter 3
Agents, Scouts, and Contracts
Navigating the Representation Maze

Welcome, rising star! Welcome to the third chapter of our epic journey through the dazzling world of modeling. Today, we're diving deep into the realm of modeling agencies, scouts, and contracts—a maze of excitement and opportunity that's waiting for you to conquer it. So let's roll up our sleeves and get ready to navigate the twists and turns of the representation game!

Decode the Mystery of Modeling Agencies and Representation

First things first, let's talk about modeling agencies—the unsung heroes of the industry! These guys are like your fairy godmothers (or godfathers) of modeling, helping you land gigs, negotiate contracts, and basically slay the game. But before you go signing on the dotted line, let's break it down:

Understanding the Role of Modeling Agencies:

Picture your modeling agency as your personal entourage—they've got your back every step of the way. From booking gigs to giving you killer career advice, these guys are your ticket to the big leagues. So choose wisely, my friend, because your agency can make all the difference in your journey to the top.

Choosing the Right Agency:

Picking the perfect agency is like finding your soulmate—it's gotta be the right fit! Do your homework, check out their reputation, and make sure they've got the connections to take your career to the next level. And hey, don't be afraid to ask around for recommendations—you never know who might have the inside scoop!

Building a Strong Relationship with Your Agent:

Once you've found your dream agency, it's time to cozy up to your agent like your favorite pair of pajamas. Keep the lines of communication open, listen to their advice, and trust that they've got your best interests at heart. After all, they're here to help you shine!

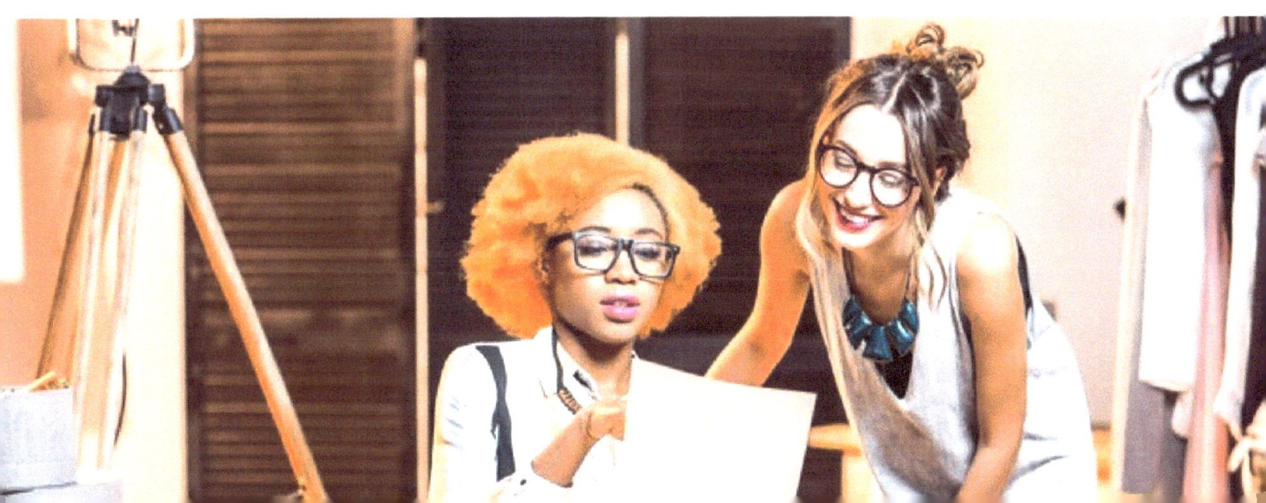

Learn the Art of Securing Your Spot in the Spotlight:

Now that you've got representation locked down, it's time to work your magic and make a splash in the modeling world. Here's how to do it:

Cultivating a Professional Image:

Repeat after me: professionalism is key! Whether you're strutting your stuff on the runway or schmoozing at a casting call, always bring your A-game and leave a lasting impression. Remember, you never know who might be watching!

Building a Strong Portfolio:

Your portfolio is your calling card in the world of modeling, so make sure it's a showstopper! Fill it with killer shots that showcase your range and versatility, and don't be afraid to switch things up to keep it fresh.

Networking and Self-Promotion:

In the world of modeling, who you know can be just as important as what you know. So get out there, mingle with industry insiders, and let your personality shine! And hey, don't forget to flex your social media muscles —Instagram, here you come!

As we wrap up our exploration of modeling agencies, scouts, and contracts, remember this: the world of modeling is a wild ride, but with the right guidance and a sprinkle of confidence, you've got what it takes to make it to the top. So go forth, my friend, and let your star shine brighter than ever before!

notes

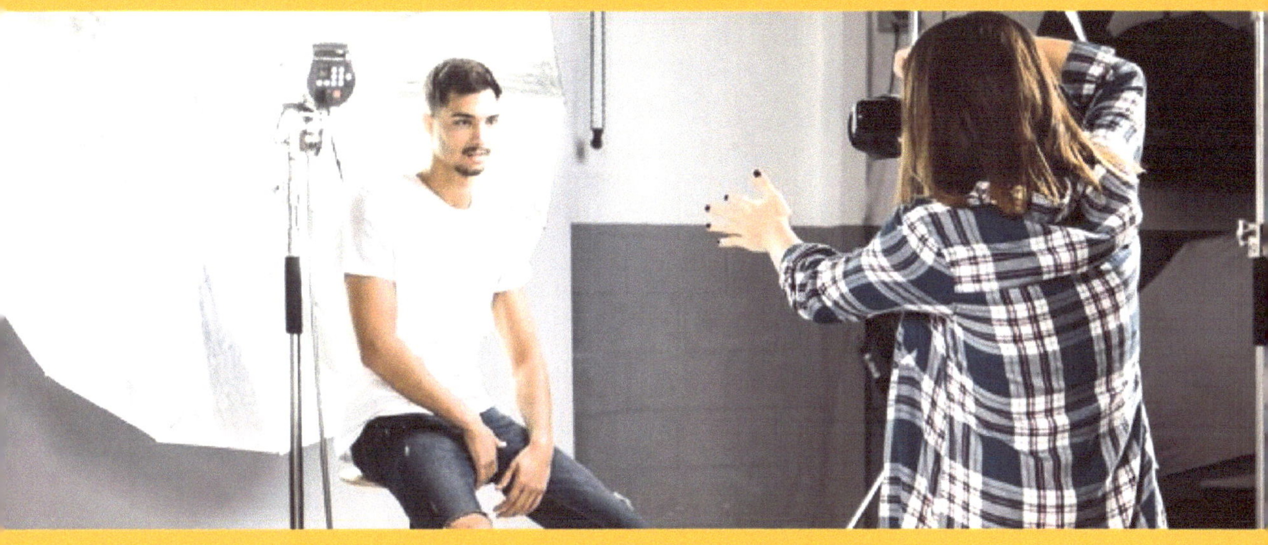

Chapter 4
Auditions Unleashed

Mastering the Art of the Casting Call

**Step onto the Stage with Confidence
Reference this Guide to Audition Success**

Alright, let's get down to business. Auditions are your time to shine, so let's make sure you're ready to knock 'em dead:

Thorough Preparation is Key:

Listen up, friend—preparation is the name of the game. Do your homework on the project or client you're auditioning for, practice your poses and runway walk until they're flawless, and show up ready to slay. Remember, confidence is key!

Dress to Impress:

You know what they say: dress for the job you want! So pick out an outfit that not only shows off your personal style but also fits the vibe of the audition. Whether it's high fashion glam or laid-back cool, make sure you look and feel like a million bucks.

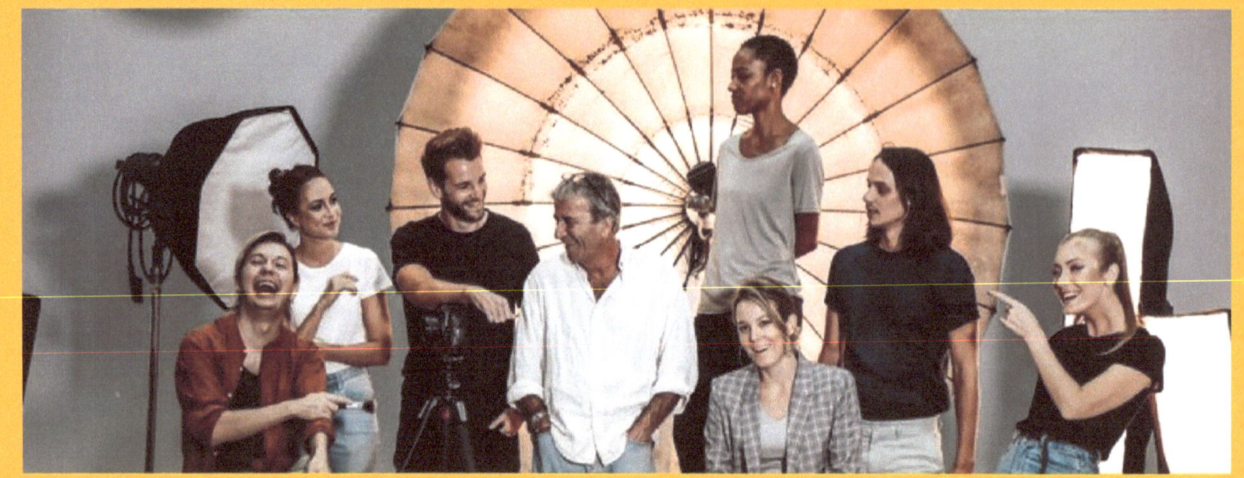

Arrive Early and Be Prepared:

Punctuality is your best friend in the world of auditions. Get to the venue with plenty of time to spare, familiarize yourself with the space, and make sure you have all your materials ready to go. Trust me, being prepared is half the battle!

Embrace Feedback and Adaptability:

Keep an open mind and be willing to take feedback on board. Auditions are all about growth and improvement, so use any feedback you receive as an opportunity to up your game. Stay flexible and adaptable, and you'll be unstoppable!

Uncover Insider Tips to Make Every Audition Your Moment to Shine

Now that you've got the basics down, let's take your audition game to the next level with some insider tips:

Showcase Your Personality:
Don't be afraid to let your personality shine through! Casting directors want to see the real you, so be genuine, engaging, and memorable. After all, it's your unique personality that will set you apart from the crowd.

Maintain Confidence and Composure:
Confidence is your secret weapon in auditions. Stand tall, speak with conviction, and own that room like it's your runway. And if nerves start to creep in, take a deep breath and remind yourself that you've got this!

Exemplify Professionalism and Respect:
Always, always, always conduct yourself with professionalism and respect. Treat everyone you encounter with kindness and courtesy, and show up prepared and ready to give it your all. Remember, you're representing yourself and your brand, so make every interaction count.

Cultivate Persistence and Resilience:
Auditioning can be tough, but don't let rejection get you down. Stay resilient, keep pushing forward, and trust that the right opportunity will come along when the time is right. Remember, every audition is a chance to learn and grow.

Model's Bag Checklist:

For Women:

1. **Portfolio or Comp Cards:** Your portfolio or comp cards are your calling cards, so make sure to have them on hand.
2. **Makeup Kit:** Include essential makeup items like foundation, concealer, mascara, and lipstick for touch-ups.
3. **Hair Accessories:** Pack hair ties, bobby pins, and hairbrush to keep your locks in place.
4. **Snacks and Water Bottle**: Stay energized and hydrated with healthy snacks and a reusable water bottle.
5. **Comfortable Flats:** Keep a pair of comfortable flats in your bag for when those heels start to pinch.
6. **Notebook and Pen**: Take notes, jot down important information, and keep track of your schedule.
7. **Portable Charger:** Ensure your devices stay charged with a portable charger.
8. **Breath Mints or Gum**: Stay fresh and confident with breath mints or gum.
9. **Emergency Sewing Kit:** Be prepared for wardrobe malfunctions with a small sewing kit.
10. **Personal Items**: Don't forget essentials like your phone, wallet, keys, and any necessary medications.

For Men:

1. **Portfolio or Comp Cards:** Have your portfolio or comp cards ready to showcase your work.
2. **Grooming Kit:** Pack grooming essentials like a comb, hair gel, and moisturizer.
3. **Breath Mints or Gum:** Keep your breath fresh with breath mints or gum.
4. **Snacks and Water Bottle:** Stay nourished and hydrated with snacks and a water bottle.
5. **Notebook and Pen**: Stay organized and jot down important information with a notebook and pen.
6. **Comfortable Shoes:** Have a pair of comfortable shoes on hand for breaks between auditions.
7. **Portable Charger:** Keep your devices charged with a portable charger.
8. **Wallet and Keys:** Don't forget your wallet and keys for any necessary transactions or access.
9. **Personal Items:** Include your phone, any necessary medications, and other personal items you may need.
10. **Headphones:** Bring headphones to relax and unwind between auditions.

notes

Chapter 5
Branding Brilliance
Carving Your Unique Identity

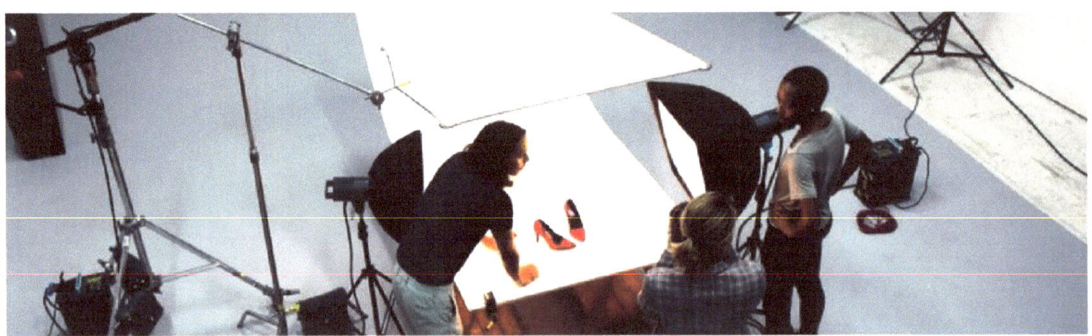

Welcome to Chapter 5 of our exhilarating journey through the world of modeling. Today, we're diving into the thrilling realm of personal branding —your ticket to standing out in a sea of stars. Let's unlock the secrets of crafting a brand that's uniquely you!

Harness the Power of Personal Branding to Stand Out in a Crowd

Alright, let's get started on crafting a brand that turns heads and leaves a lasting impression:

Define Your Unique Identity:

First things first, what makes you, well, you? Take a moment to reflect on your strengths, passions, and values. Whether it's your killer runway walk or your commitment to sustainability, embrace the qualities that set you apart and form the foundation of your personal brand.

Identify Your Target Audience:

Who are you trying to reach with your brand? Fashionistas, fitness enthusiasts, commercial clients? Get to know your audience inside and out, and tailor your branding efforts to meet their needs and desires. The better you understand your audience, the more impactful your branding will be.

Craft a Compelling Brand Story:

Every brand has a story, and yours should be nothing short of captivating. Share your journey, aspirations, and values in a way that resonates with authenticity and emotion. Your brand story should draw people in, forge connections, and leave them wanting more.

Curate Your Visual Identity:

Your visual identity is the face of your brand, so make sure it's a memorable one. From your portfolio to your social media posts, ensure consistency in elements like color palette, typography, and imagery. Your visual identity should reflect your personality and values at every turn.

WEEK 1:

- Monday: Introduction - Share a fun fact about yourself or your content niche.
- Tuesday: Behind the Scenes - Show your audience what goes into creating your content.
- Wednesday: Q&A - Answer questions from your followers or audience.
- Thursday: Throwback - Share a throwback post or highlight an older piece of content.
- Friday: Collaboration - Feature another content creator or brand you admire.
- Saturday: Tutorial - Share a how-to tutorial related to your content niche.
- Sunday: Weekly Recap - Summarize the week's highlights and upcoming content.

WEEK 2:

- Monday: Motivation Monday - Share an inspirational quote or story.
- Tuesday: Trending Topic - Discuss a current trend or topic relevant to your niche.
- Wednesday: Product Review - Review a product related to your content niche.
- Thursday: Throwback - Share a throwback post or highlight an older piece of content.
- Friday: Fun Fact - Share an interesting fact or trivia related to your niche.
- Saturday: Challenge - Start a challenge for your audience to participate in.
- Sunday: Self-care Sunday - Share tips or practices for self-care and wellness.

WEEK 3:

- Monday: Ask Me Anything - Encourage your audience to ask you anything.
- Tuesday: Trending Topic - Discuss a current trend or topic relevant to your niche.
- Wednesday: Behind the Scenes - Show your audience what goes into creating your content.
- Thursday: Throwback - Share a throwback post or highlight an older piece of content.
- Friday: Collaboration - Feature another content creator or brand you admire.
- Saturday: Tutorial - Share a how-to tutorial related to your content niche.
- Sunday: Weekly Recap - Summarize the week's highlights and upcoming content.

WEEK 4:

- Monday: Motivation Monday - Share an inspirational quote or story.
- Tuesday: Trending Topic - Discuss a current trend or topic relevant to your niche.
- Wednesday: Product Review - Review a product related to your content niche.
- Thursday: Throwback - Share a throwback post or highlight an older piece of content.
- Friday: Fun Fact - Share an interesting fact or trivia related to your niche.
- Saturday: Challenge - Start a challenge for your audience to participate in.
- Sunday: Self-care Sunday - Share tips or practices for self-care and wellness.

Month 1:
- Weeks 1-4: Focus on Introductions, Behind the Scenes, Q&A, Throwbacks, Collaborations, Tutorials, and Weekly Recaps.

Month 2:
- Weeks 5-8: Continue with Motivation Monday, Trending Topics, Product Reviews, Fun Facts, Challenges, and Self-care Sundays. Introduce more interactive content like polls or quizzes.

Month 3:
- Weeks 9-12: Further engage your audience with Ask Me Anything sessions, additional Trending Topics, more Behind the Scenes content, and increased emphasis on collaborations. Incorporate user-generated content or testimonials.

- Throughout the 90-day period, consistently monitor engagement metrics and adjust your content strategy accordingly. Experiment with different content formats, posting times, and frequency to optimize audience reach and engagement.

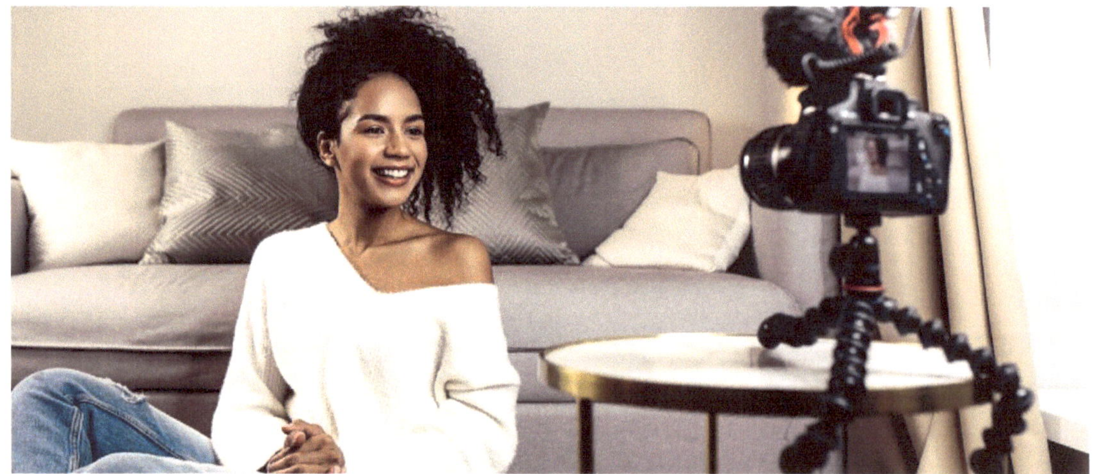

Chapter 6

Networking Like a Pro
The Art of Making Connections

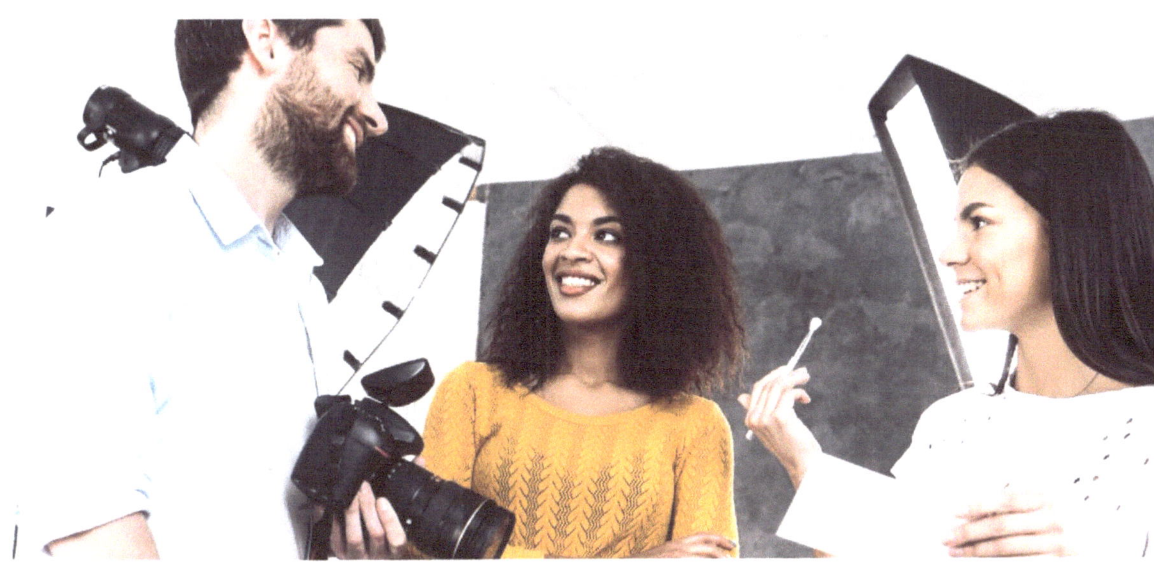

Navigate the Social Scene with Finesse: Networking Tips for Models

Here are some key strategies to help you navigate the social landscape with finesse:

- **Embrace Authenticity:**

Be yourself! Authenticity is key to making genuine connections that last. Approach interactions with sincerity and a genuine desire to get to know others.

- **Hone Small Talk Skills:**

Master the art of small talk—it's your ticket to deeper connections. Start with light-hearted conversations and gradually transition into more meaningful dialogues.

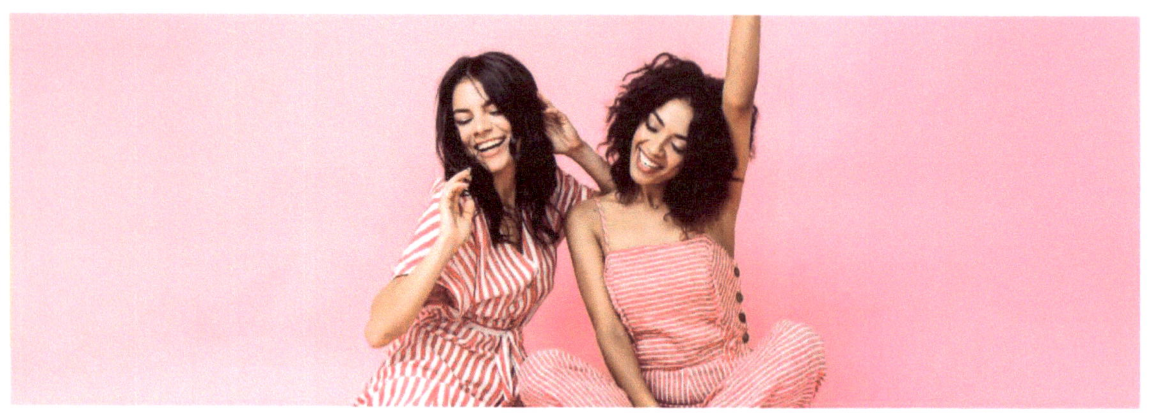

NETWORKING EVENTS IN MY AREA:

- [Event Name] - Date: [Insert Date], Location: [Insert Location]
- [Event Name] - Date: [Insert Date], Location: [Insert Location]
- [Event Name] - Date: [Insert Date], Location: [Insert Location]
- [Event Name] - Date: [Insert Date], Location: [Insert Location]
- [Event Name] - Date: [Insert Date], Location: [Insert Location]

CASTING CALLS IN MY AREA:

-
- [Project Name] - Date: [Insert Date], Location: [Insert Location], Contact: [Insert Contact Info]
- [Project Name] - Date: [Insert Date], Location: [Insert Location], Contact: [Insert Contact Info]
- [Project Name] - Date: [Insert Date], Location: [Insert Location], Contact: [Insert Contact Info]
- [Project Name] - Date: [Insert Date], Location: [Insert Location], Contact: [Insert Contact Info]
- [Project Name] - Date: [Insert Date], Location: [Insert Location], Contact: [Insert Contact Info]

Forge Lasting Connections That Elevate Your Career

Now, let's explore how to forge lasting connections that will take your career to the next level:

- **Craft a Compelling Personal Brand**: Define your unique identity as a model and communicate it effectively across all platforms. Your personal brand should resonate with your target audience and set you apart from the competition.

- **Stay Informed and Engaged:** Stay up-to-date with industry trends and developments to demonstrate your commitment to excellence. Engage with industry publications and social media channels to stay informed.

- **Diversify Your Network:** Connect with professionals from diverse backgrounds and sectors within the industry. Collaborate with individuals who offer fresh perspectives and complementary skills.

- **Prioritize Long-Term Relationships**: Invest time and effort in nurturing enduring relationships with industry professionals. Sustained relationships often lead to lasting opportunities and collaborations.

- **Exemplify Reliability and Excellence:** Consistently deliver excellence in your work and maintain a reputation for reliability and professionalism. Your reputation as a trusted collaborator will open doors to new opportunities.

- **Embrace Collaborative Opportunities**: Seek out opportunities to collaborate with other models, photographers, and creatives on projects that showcase your skills and amplify your impact.

- **Champion Continuous Growth**: Embrace a mindset of continuous learning and growth throughout your career. Seek feedback, pursue learning opportunities, and embrace challenges as opportunities for development.

- **Celebrate Collective Success:** Acknowledge and celebrate the achievements of your peers, fostering a supportive and collaborative environment within the industry.

- **Cultivate Resilience:** Stay resilient in the face of challenges and setbacks. Maintain a positive outlook and persevere with determination, knowing that every obstacle is an opportunity for growth.

- **Give Back to Society:** Use your platform and influence to make a positive impact in the world. Volunteer your time, raise awareness for important causes, and advocate for meaningful change.

Networking is an essential skill for success in the modeling industry. By approaching networking with authenticity, building lasting connections, and prioritizing continuous growth, you'll position yourself for long-term success and fulfillment in your career. So go ahead, make those connections, and watch your career soar!

notes

notes

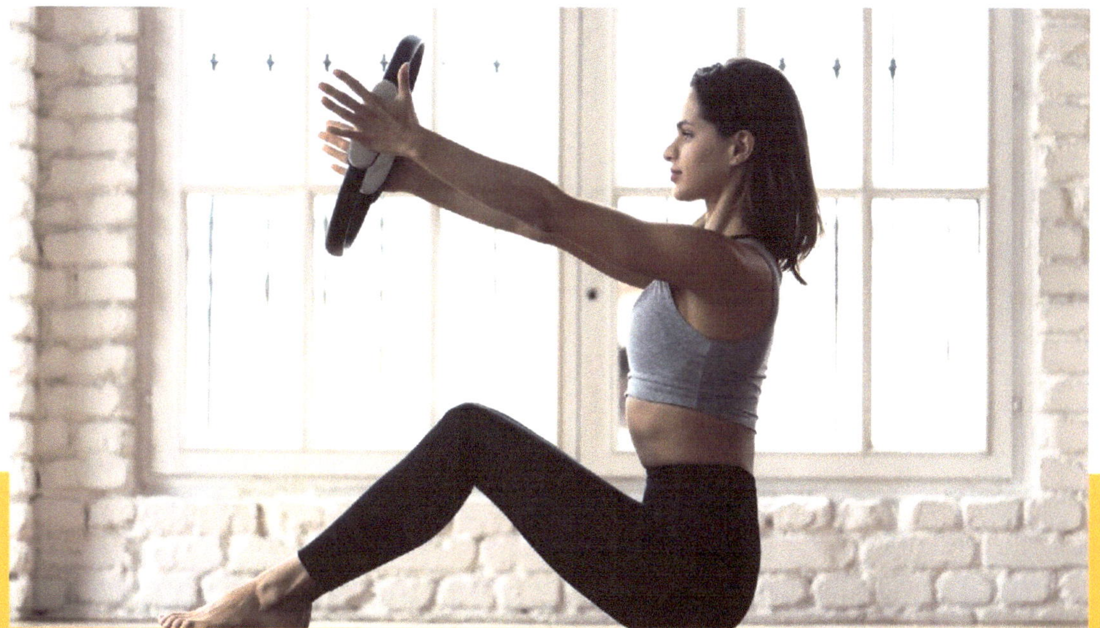

Chapter 7
Striking a Balance
The Model's Guide to Health and Wellness

Embrace Self-Care as a Vital Ingredient for Success

Self-care is not just a luxury—it's a necessity for success in the modeling industry. Here's how you can prioritize self-care:

1. Prioritize Rest and Recovery:

Make sure you're getting enough sleep each night to replenish your energy levels and promote overall well-being. Incorporate restorative practices like meditation or gentle yoga into your routine to combat stress.

2. Nourish Your Body:

Fuel your body with nutrient-dense foods that support optimal health. Focus on incorporating a variety of fruits, vegetables, lean proteins, whole grains, and healthy fats into your diet. Stay hydrated by drinking plenty of water throughout the day.

3. Engage in Regular Exercise:

Physical activity is essential for maintaining a strong, healthy body. Find activities you enjoy, such as dancing or swimming, and make them a regular part of your routine.

4. Practice Mindfulness:

Cultivate mindfulness practices like meditation or deep breathing exercises to foster mental clarity and emotional resilience. Take time each day to connect with yourself and promote inner peace.

5. Set Boundaries:

Establish clear boundaries to protect your physical and emotional well-being. Learn to say no to commitments that drain your energy and prioritize activities that nourish you.

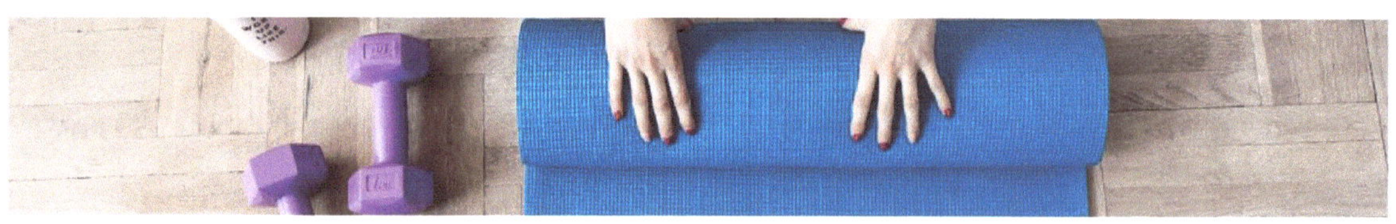

Discover Strategies to Keep Your Body and Mind in Peak Condition

Here are some additional strategies to keep your body and mind in top shape:

1. Prioritize Regular Health Check-Ups:
Schedule regular check-ups with healthcare professionals to monitor your physical health and address any issues early on.

2. Practice Safe Modeling Practices:
Advocate for safe working conditions on shoots and runway shows. Be mindful of the risks associated with certain modeling practices and prioritize your health above all else.

3. Invest in Proper Nutrition and Hydration:
Fuel your body with a balanced diet and stay hydrated throughout the day, especially during busy days of casting calls and photo shoots.

4. Incorporate Regular Exercise:
Make physical activity a regular part of your routine to maintain strength, flexibility, and cardiovascular health.

5. Practice Stress Management Techniques:
Develop effective stress management techniques to cope with the demands of the industry and maintain emotional well-being.

notes

Chapter 8
Dollars and Sense
Financial Fitness for Models

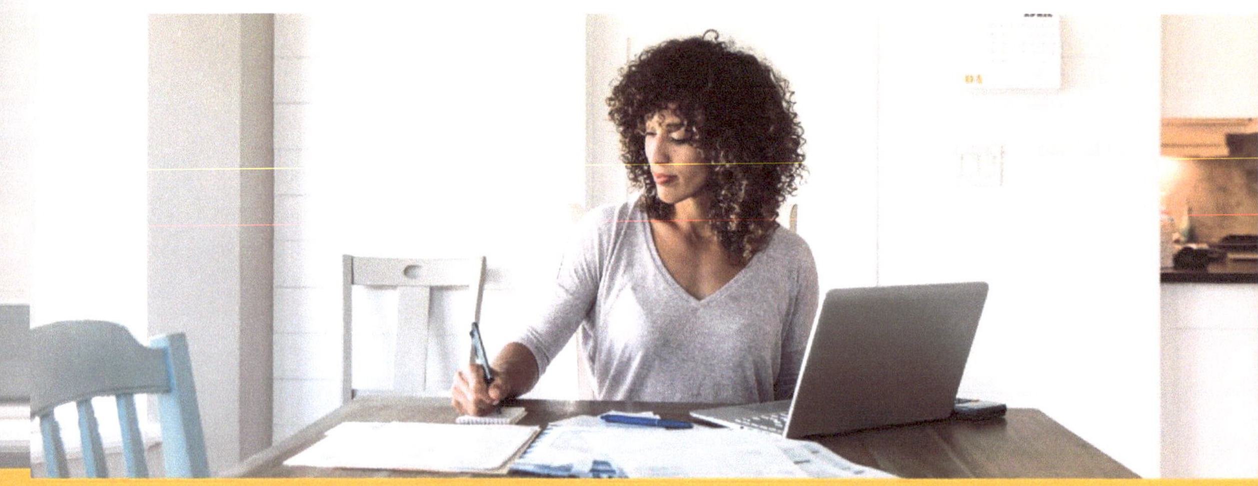

Navigate the Financial Landscape of Modeling with Confidence

- **Know Your Worth:** You're valuable, so make sure you get paid what you deserve. Do your research, negotiate confidently, and advocate for fair compensation.

- **Diversify Your Income:** Modeling gigs can be unpredictable, so explore other opportunities like endorsements or entrepreneurship to keep your cash flow steady.

- **Budget Wisely:** Create a budget that fits your lifestyle and goals. Keep track of your spending and make sure to save for the things that matter most.

- **Save for Taxes:** Don't forget about taxes! Set aside money from each paycheck so you're not caught off guard come tax time.

- **Invest in Your Future:** Start planning for retirement early by investing in retirement accounts. Your future self will thank you!

Master the Art of Money Management and Secure Your Financial Future

Set Clear Financial Goals: What do you want to achieve financially? Whether it's buying a house or traveling the world, set clear goals and make a plan to reach them.

Track Your Income and Expenses: Keep tabs on your money to see where it's going. Budgeting tools and apps can help you stay on top of your finances.

Live Within Your Means: Avoid overspending and prioritize your needs over wants. Living within your means will keep your finances in check.

Manage Debt Wisely: Don't let debt weigh you down. Pay off high-interest debt first and be strategic about managing your loans.

Invest Strategically: Grow your money by investing wisely. Diversify your portfolio and work with a financial advisor if needed.

Monitor Your Credit: Keep an eye on your credit score and report to maintain good financial health. Good credit opens doors to better opportunities.

Plan for Major Expenses: Anticipate big expenses like taxes or healthcare costs and budget for them accordingly.

Stay Flexible and Adapt: Life is unpredictable, so be prepared to adjust your financial plans as needed. Stay flexible and keep moving forward.

Balance Sheet: Income and Paid Jobs

Source of Income / Paid Jobs	Amount ($)	Date Received / Paid
Runway Show	1000	2024-03-15
Photoshoot	800	2024-03-20
Endorsement	1200	2024-03-25
Social Media Collaboration	500	2024-04-05
Casting Call	600	2024-04-10
Total Income / Paid Jobs	**$4100.00**	

Balance Sheet: Expenses

Expense	Amount ($)	Date Paid
Gas	100	2024-03-01
Meals	300	2024-03-05
Modeling Supplies	150	2024-03-10
Makeup	100	2024-03-15
Studio Set up	200	2024-03-20
Camera	150	2024-03-25
Total Expenses	**$1000.00**	

Your Journey Begins Now

Congratulations, fellow model! You're about to embark on an incredible journey in the thrilling world of modeling, and let me tell you, the adventure ahead is nothing short of exhilarating. From the glitz and glam of runway shows to the behind-the-scenes hustle of casting calls, your path is paved with excitement, challenges, and boundless opportunities.

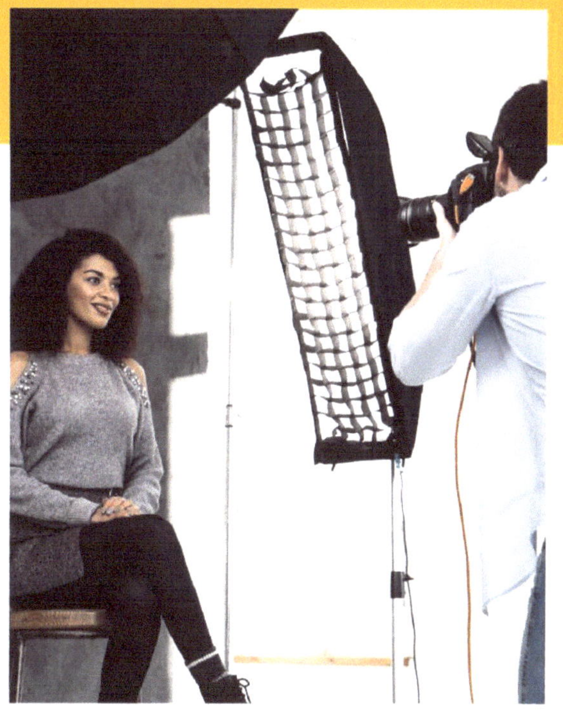

As you dive headfirst into this whirlwind of experiences, I urge you to embrace it all with an open heart and a fearless spirit. Yes, there will be highs and lows, triumphs and setbacks, but each moment holds valuable lessons and the potential for tremendous growth. Remember, success in this industry isn't just about talent and determination—it's about resilience, adaptability, and unwavering self-belief.

Now, as you gear up for the journey ahead, consider creating your very own Model Handbook To-Do List to keep you focused and on track. Here's a sneak peek at what you might include:

Define Your Goals: Take some time to map out your dreams and aspirations in the modeling world. Whether it's gracing the cover of a magazine or strutting your stuff on the catwalk, clarity is key to making your dreams a reality.

Invest in Your Craft: Never stop learning and growing. Seek out opportunities to refine your skills and stay ahead of the curve. Workshops, classes, and seminars are your best friends in this regard.

Build Your Portfolio: Your portfolio is your calling card, so make it shine! Collaborate with talented creatives to capture your essence and showcase your versatility. Remember, variety is the spice of life (and portfolios).

Network with Purpose: Cultivate meaningful connections with industry insiders and fellow models. Attend events, engage on social media, and don't be afraid to reach out to potential mentors. You never know where your next opportunity might come from!

Take Care of Yourself: Your well-being is non-negotiable. Make self-care a priority, both physically and mentally. You'll thank yourself later, trust me.

Stay Persistent and Resilient: The road to success isn't always smooth, but with perseverance and a positive attitude, you can overcome any obstacle that comes your way. Keep pushing forward, and never lose sight of your goals.

Celebrate Your Achievements: Big or small, every achievement deserves to be celebrated. Take pride in your hard work and accomplishments, and let them fuel your determination to reach even greater heights.

Remain Humble and Grateful: Last but certainly not least, always remember to stay humble and grateful. You're living your dream in an industry filled with countless aspiring talents. Never take that for granted.

So, my fellow model, are you ready to embark on this incredible journey? I have no doubt that you'll conquer the runway (and the world) with style, grace, and an unshakeable sense of purpose. Here's to the adventure of a lifetime—let's make every moment count